Heath Social Studies
Homes and Neighborhoods

HEATH

Program Authors

Gloria P. Hagans Social Studies Coordinator, K–12, Norfolk Public Schools, Norfolk, Virginia.

Barbara Radner Reque Director, DePaul University Center for Economic Education, Chicago, Illinois.

Richard Hall Wilson Social Studies Coordinator, Montgomery County Public Schools, Rockville, Maryland; Instructor, American History, University of Maryland and Montgomery College.

Reading Consultants

Ted Schuder Coordinator, K–8 Reading/Language Arts Program, Montgomery County Public Schools, Rockville, Maryland.

Nan Jackson Reading/Language Arts Specialist, Montgomery County Public Schools, Rockville, Maryland.

Executive Editor Phyllis Goldstein
Freelance Assistance Susan T. Marx
Editorial Services Marianna Frew Palmer
Series Designer Robert H. Botsford

Reviewers

Virginia M. Bryant Social Studies Coordinator, Pascagoula (Mississippi) Municipal Separate School District.

Leah Engelhardt Professor, Curriculum and Instruction, Mississippi State University.

Nancy N. Galante Curriculum Specialist, Broward County (Florida) Public Schools.

Sandra Pressler Teacher, Port Wentworth School, Port Wentworth, Georgia.

James H. Rogers Former Social Studies Supervisor, Broward County (Florida) Public Schools.

Heath Social Studies

Homes and Neighborhoods

Barbara Radner Reque

D.C. Heath and Company
Lexington, Massachusetts   Toronto

Published simultaneously in Canada

Printed in the United States of America

International Standard Book Number: 0-669-11385-9

2 3 4 5 6 7 8 9 0

Contents

Unit Seven
Holidays around the World 125

Maps

Graphs, Charts, and Diagrams

Unit One
The Earth You Live On

You live on **Earth.**
Earth has land.
It has water.
It has air.

Land

Land is part of Earth.
Some land is high.

⑩

Some land is low.

11

People use land.
How do people use land?

Water

Water is part of Earth.

Water is in this **river.**

Water is in this **lake.**

This is an **ocean.**
Most water is in oceans.
Oceans are very, very big.

15

People use water.
How do people use water?

Air

Air is everywhere on Earth.
People breathe air.
Air moves.
Wind is moving air.
How do people use the wind?

This is a **globe.**
A globe shows Earth.

A globe shows land.
What color is the land?

A globe shows water.
What color is the water?

North Pole

South Pole

Look at the globe on this page.
Find the North Pole.

Put your finger somewhere on the globe.
Now move your finger toward the North Pole.
You are going north.

Now move your finger toward the South Pole.
In which direction are you going?

Wet or Dry
Cold or Hot

Some land is wet.
It gets much rain.
What lives there?

Some land is dry.
It does not get much rain.
What lives there?

23

Some places are cold all year.
What lives in cold places?

24

Some places are hot all year.
What lives in hot places?

Seasons

Some places change.
Sometimes they are cold.

Fall

Winter

Sometimes they are hot.

Spring

Summer

Living in Many Places

People live in many places.

You live in a place.
What is it like?

Unit Review

Words to Know

Match the words to the pictures.

Earth   ocean   lake   water

land   wind   river   globe

30

Reviewing Main Ideas

Draw pictures to show what you do.

1. How do you use land?

2. How do you use water?

3. How do you use air?

Keeping Skills Sharp

1. What does a globe show?

2. What does the yellow show?

3. What does the blue show?

4. What does north mean?

Challenge!

Read the clues.

Then guess the season.

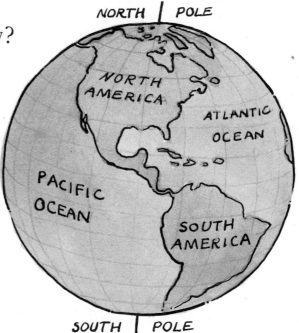

It is hot.

Some people swim in a lake.

Some people go to the ocean.

Can you give clues about another season?

Have someone else guess the season.

Unit Two
Families

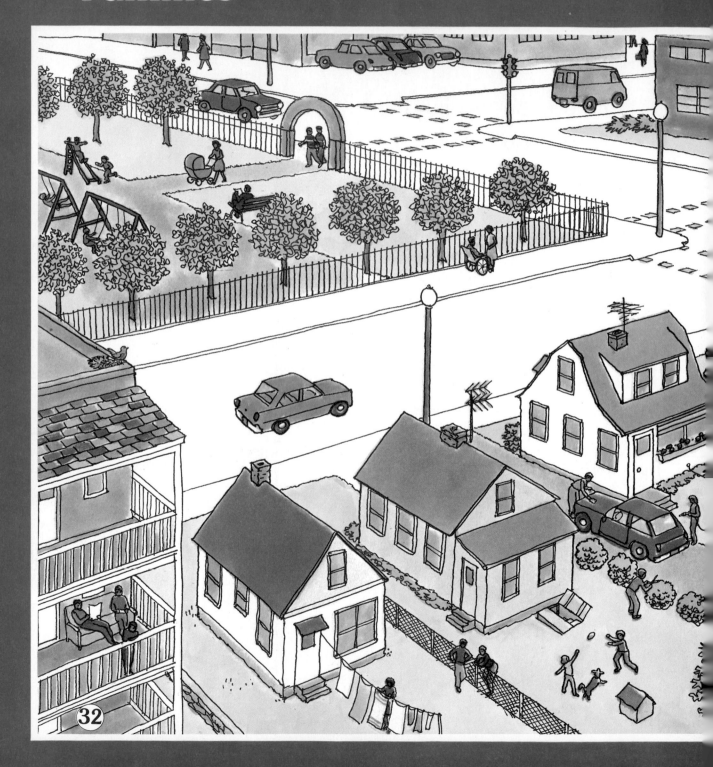

You are part of a **family**.
Everywhere on Earth there are families.
Find the families in this picture.

33

Many Families

Families live in many ways.
They do things together.

Many Homes

Your family lives in a **home**.
Families live in many kinds of homes.

North

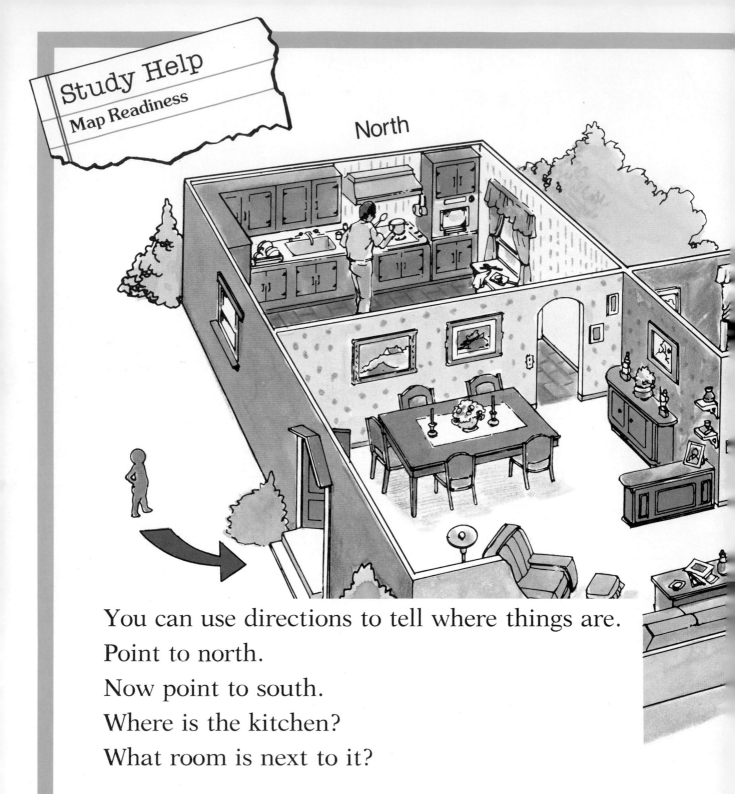

You can use directions to tell where things are.

Point to north.

Now point to south.

Where is the kitchen?

What room is next to it?

Find Jennifer's room.
Where is it?
Where is Mike's room?

Meeting Needs

All families need things.
They need a home.
What else do they need?

41

Working

Families need **money** to buy things.
People **work.**
They have jobs.
People earn money.

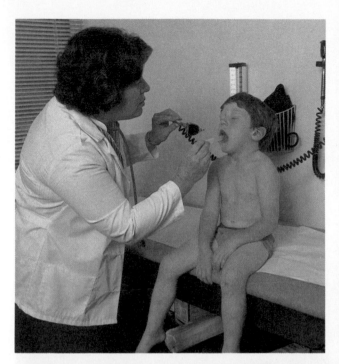

Helping

Families do things together.
Look at this family.
What jobs does the family do?
Everybody helps.

A Birthday Party

Today is a special day for the family.

It is a birthday.

The family gets ready for the party.

How does the family share the work?

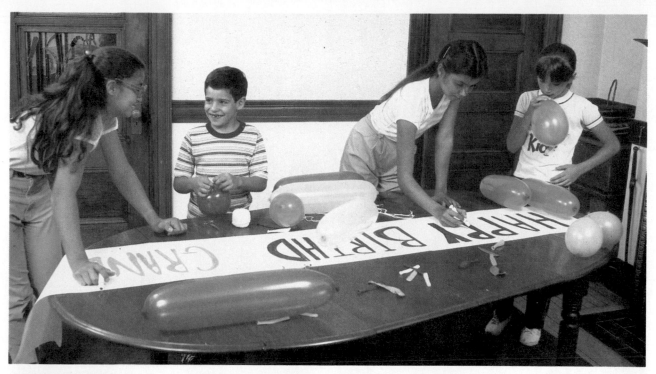

47

This is the birthday party.
Whom is the party for?

How does the family share the fun?

Unit Review

Words to Know

Match the words to the pictures.

family
home
work
money

Reviewing Main Ideas

Name three things that families need.
Tell how children can help families.

Keeping Skills Sharp

Look at these homes.

1. How are they the same?

2. How are they different?

Challenge!

Make pictures of people in a family.

Cut out the pictures.

Put them on sticks.

Put on a puppet show.

Unit Three
The Neighborhood

People live near you.
They are your neighbors.
You are part of a **neighborhood**.

53

Neighbors

Neighbors live near each other.
They share the same streets.
What else do neighbors share?

56

Neighbors share this park.
They have fun in it.
They also take care of it.

The Fire House

Many people work in the neighborhood.
This is a **fire house.**
These workers put out fires.
What do you see in the fire house?
What can you do to help these workers?

The Police

The **police** help people.
They help people follow rules.

The police help children cross streets.
They help keep people safe.

The Library

Some people work in the **library.**
They help children find books.
What else do they do?

A **map** is a drawing of a place.

There are colors, lines, dots, or pictures on a map.

They stand for real things.

This is a map of Amy's neighborhood.

A key helps you read a map.

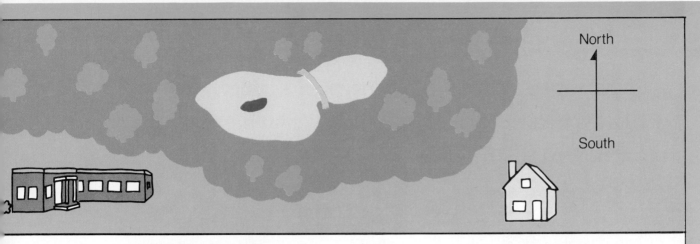

Green Street

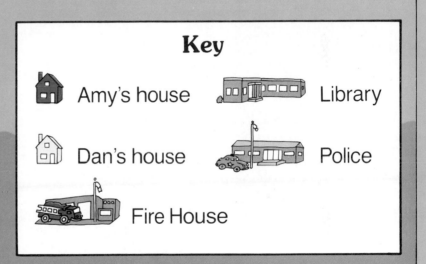

Key

Amy's house

Library

Dan's house

Police

Fire House

Look at the key.

Find Amy's house in the key.

Now find Amy's house on the map.

Who is her neighbor?

On what street is the library?

The Post Office

Many people work for the **post office.**
They take letters to people everywhere.
A boy mails a letter.
Where does it go?

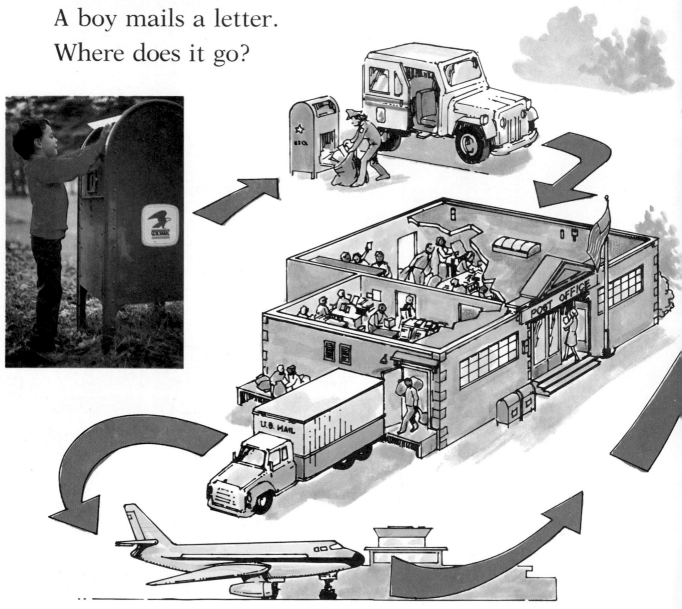

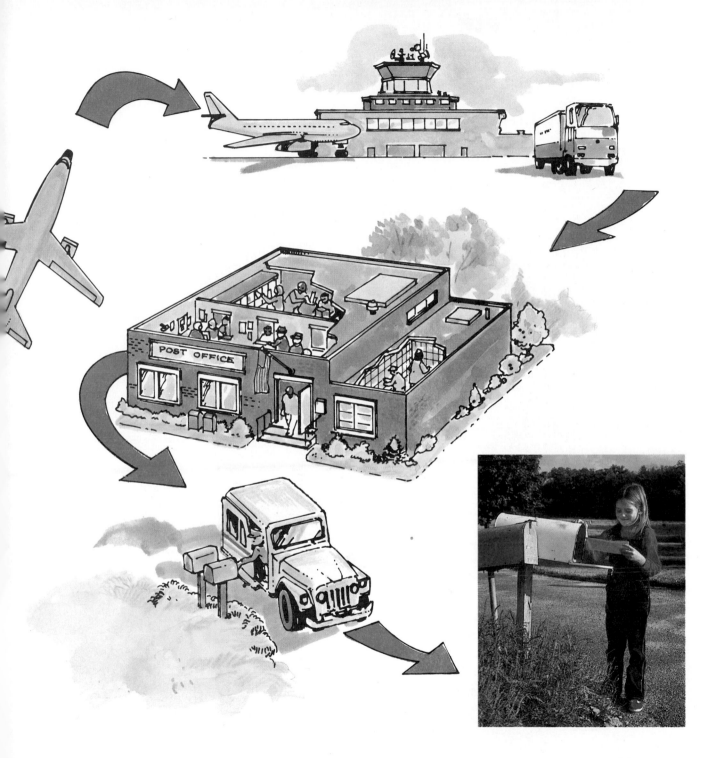

Unit Review

Words to Know

1. Tell who works in a neighborhood.

2. What is a map?

Reviewing Main Ideas

Who are some workers in your neighborhood?
Draw a picture showing some workers.

Keeping Skills Sharp

1. What helps you read a map?

2. What is next to the fire house?

3. On what street is the post office?

4. What will you find on Second Avenue?

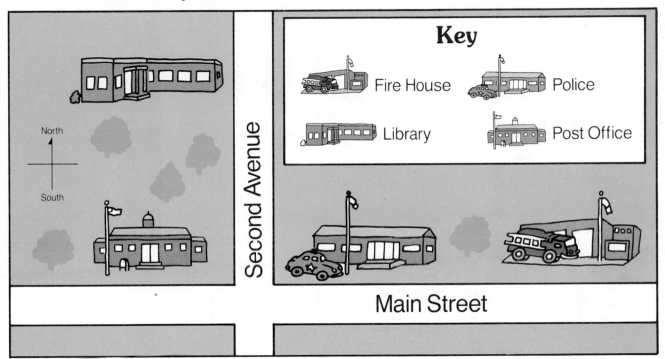

Challenge!

What is in your neighborhood?

What do you see on your way to school?

Show the places on your own map.

Unit Four
School

You go to **school.**
Other children go there too.
What can you do at school?

Using Words

Children learn in school.
They learn to use words.

They read.

They write.

They talk and listen.

Using Numbers

Children learn numbers in school.

They count.   They add.

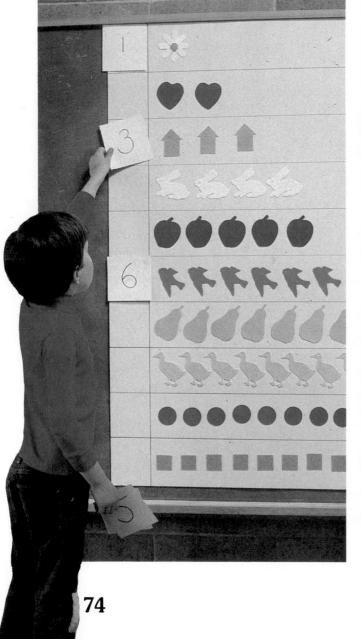

How do you use numbers?

Learning Other Things

Children paint pictures in school.

They sing with other children.

They hop.
They jump.
They run.

Children use maps.

They learn sign language.

They learn about animals.

They ask questions.

The children work in school.

They learn to read.

When do they read?

What do they do next?

What do they do at 12 o'clock?
What do they do at 1 o'clock?
Where do they go at 3 o'clock?

Learning from Many People

Children learn in many places.
They learn from many people too.
Where are the children learning?

83

Learning at Home

Children learn from their families.
What are these children learning?

Unit Review

Words to Know

Find the word to finish the last sentence.
Then write the sentences on your paper.

Children add numbers.   maps
Children read words.   school
Children learn in _____.   pictures

Reviewing Main Ideas

1. Name four things you
   learn in school.

2. Name four things you
   learn at home.

Keeping Skills Sharp

The children go on a trip.

1. What do they do first?

2. What do they do at 10 o'clock?

3. What do the children do last?

Challenge!

Look at the chart on this page.

Make your own chart.

Show your day at school.

88

You use many things.
They come from near and far.

89

Gardens

Some people grow food.
They have gardens.
What food grows in this garden?

91

Farms

This is a **farm.**

Most food comes from farms.

Some farmers raise animals.

Some grow plants.

Growing Wheat

Bread starts on a farm.
It starts as wheat.

First, farmers plant wheat.

The wheat grows and grows.

Then farmers cut the wheat.

Where does the wheat go next?

The Flour Mill

The wheat goes to a **factory.**
Workers make things in a factory.
This factory is called a flour mill.

Workers there make wheat into flour.
They use big machines.

A truck takes the flour.
It goes far away.
Guess where it goes.

The Bakery

The flour goes to the bakery.
The bakery is a factory too.
Workers make bread there.
They use flour to make the bread.

The bread goes to the store.
Who buys the bread?
Who eats it?
You do!

99

Children in Jill's class had a vote.

They voted on the kind of bread they like best.

The children wanted to show how they voted.

They made a graph.

A graph can help you compare things.

Look at the graph.

What kinds of bread did they vote for?

How many voted for whole wheat bread?

What kind of bread do most children like best?
What kind of bread do the children like least?

Unit Review

Words to Know

Make a picture for each word.
Show what people do there.

    factory   farm

Reviewing Main Ideas

Look at each picture.
What happens first?
What happens next?
What happens last?

Keeping Skills Sharp

1. How many cows are on Susan's farm?

2. Which farm has three cows?

3. Which farm has the most cows?

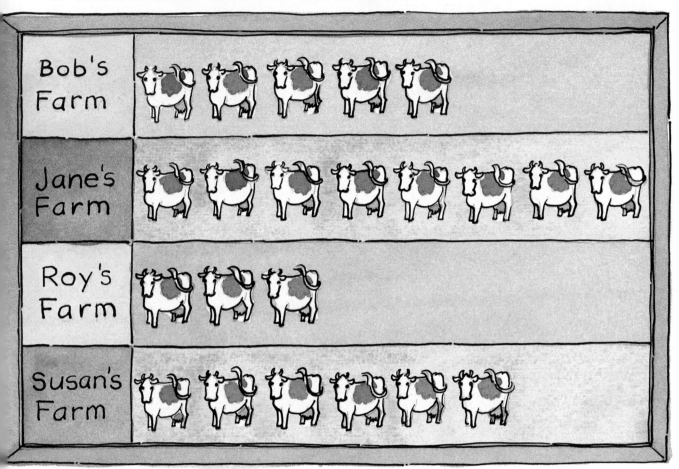

Challenge!

Ask your class to vote on a favorite vegetable.

Make a graph to show how the class voted.

Unit Six
Shopping Center

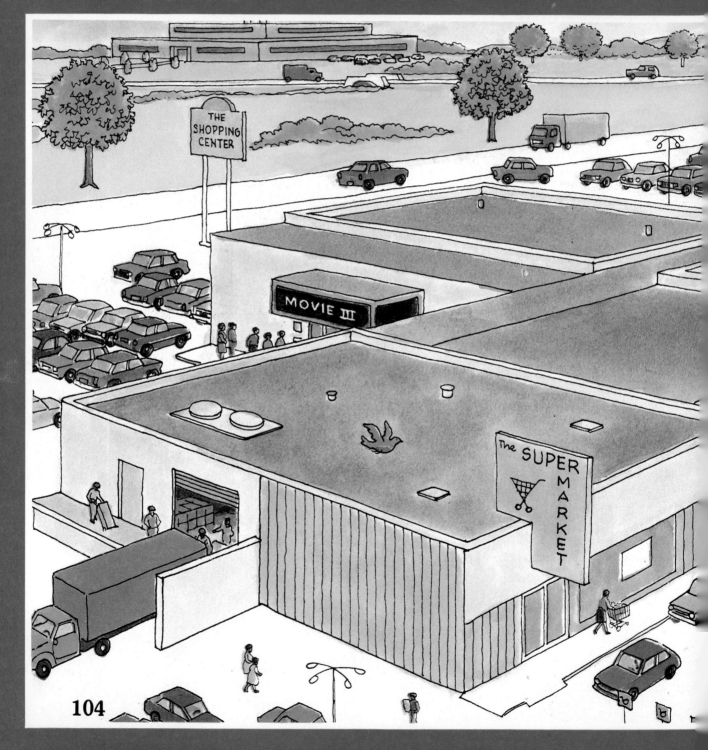

You buy things in a **store.**
A **shopping center** has many stores.
What could you buy in these stores?

105

This is a map of a shopping center.
The map shows where the stores are.

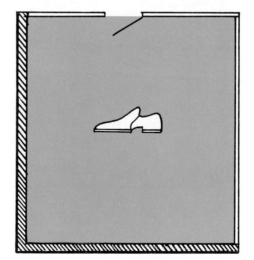

Start at the ⊗ .

Go to the .

Turn right.

Go to the .

Turn left.

Go to the .

Go into the store.

What can you buy there?

⊗
You
are
here.

106

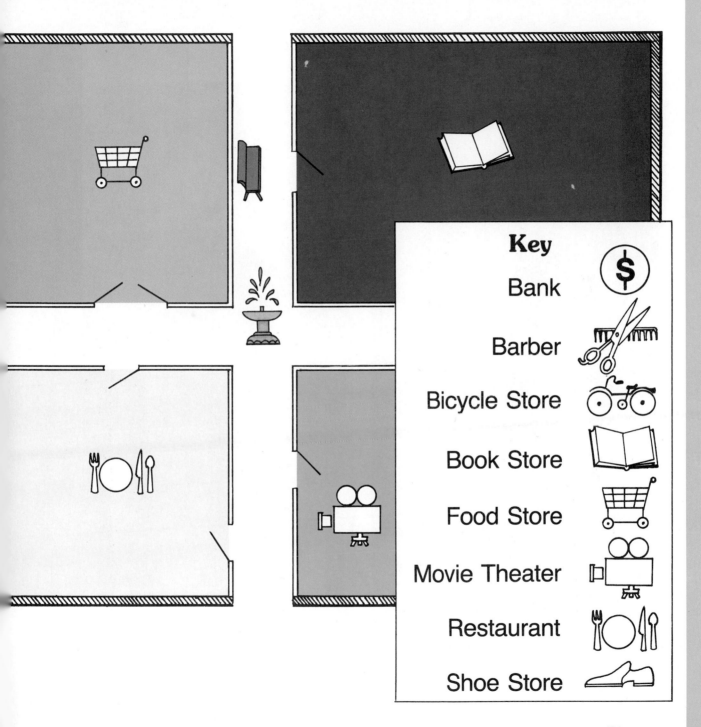

Key

Bank

Barber

Bicycle Store

Book Store

Food Store

Movie Theater

Restaurant

Shoe Store

Many Workers

There are many jobs in the stores.

Some workers bring things into the stores.
What else do workers do?

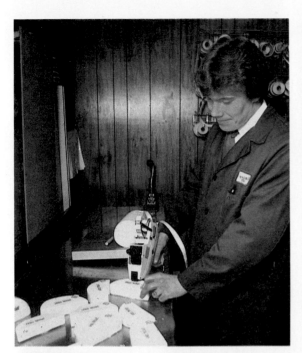

Some workers do things for the family.

They cut hair.

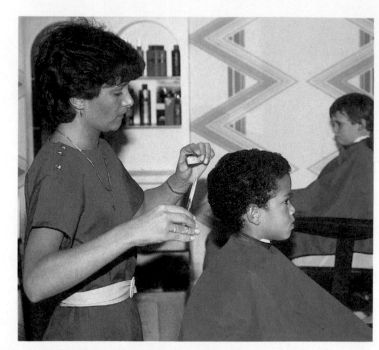

They fix things.

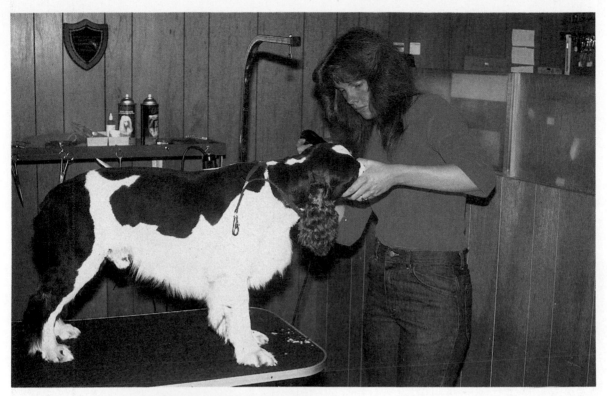

They take care of pets.

They cook food.

111

At the Bicycle Store

A boy goes to a store.
His bicycle does not work.
What does it need?

Should the boy buy a new one?
Should he have it fixed?

At the Shoe Store

A girl needs shoes.

She wants shoes for running.

Her mother wants the shoes to last.

The clerk helps them.

At the Bank

A family goes to the **bank.**
Workers there help people.

People save money at a bank.
They borrow money too.

Having a Good Time

People have fun at the shopping center.

They eat food.

They see a movie.

A man does tricks.
People watch the show.

A woman makes a picture.
The girl likes it.

People get together everywhere on Earth.

They buy and sell.

They visit friends.

They have a good time.

120

Unit Review

Words to Know

Find the right word to finish each sentence.
Then write the sentences on your paper.

People save money in a _____.   store

People buy things in a _____.   shopping center

People find many stores in a _____. bank

Reviewing Main Ideas

What do these workers do?
How do they help us?

Keeping Skills Sharp

Tell  how to get to the store.

1. What street should 🚶 go on first?

2. Where should 🚶 turn?

3. Should 🚶 turn left or right?

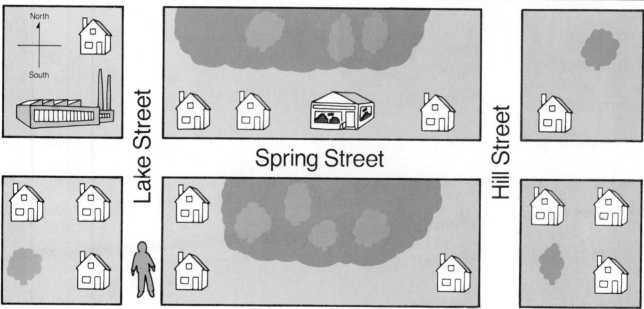

Challenge!

Use the map above to help you.

1. How many homes are there?

2. On what street is the factory?

3. What is to the right of the store?

This is a holiday.
It is a happy time.
People are having fun together.

125

Remembering Long Ago

Long ago Christopher Columbus set sail.
He and his men had three small ships.

They went a long, long way.
They sailed across the ocean.
At last they came to the Americas.
We remember this trip on Columbus Day.

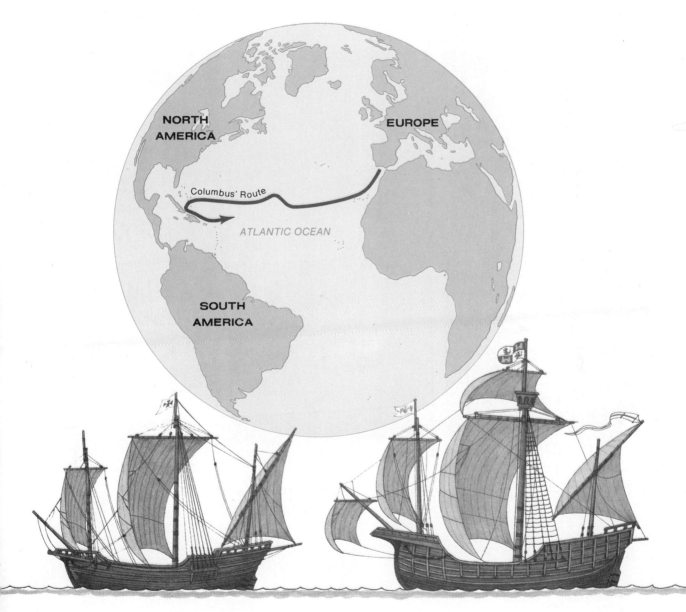

NORTH
AMERICA

EUROPE

Columbus' Route

ATLANTIC OCEAN

SOUTH
AMERICA

Harvest Time

It is fall.
Food is ready for the winter.
Many people give thanks.

The Pilgrims gave thanks for their friends.
The Pilgrims gave thanks for homes and food.
Today we give thanks too.

Starting a New Year

Last year is over.
A new year begins.

We start a new calendar.
Sometimes people have big parties.

Sometimes people have parades.

Remembering Our Leaders

Martin Luther King, Jr., had a dream.
He wanted every person to have a good life.
He wanted people to live as neighbors.
We remember his birthday.

Abraham Lincoln was born in a cabin.
When he grew up, Lincoln was president.
He wanted all Americans to be free.
We also remember Lincoln on his birthday.

134

George Washington lived long ago.

He helped our country in many ways.

He helped our country to become free.

He helped to write our country's rules.

He was the first president.

We remember Washington on his birthday.

In Spring

Spring is a time for fun outside.
In Japan people look at cherry blossoms.

Many people plant trees.

These children live in Israel.
They are planting trees.
It is the New Year of Trees.

It is Arbor Day in our country.
These people buy a tree.
Then they will plant it.

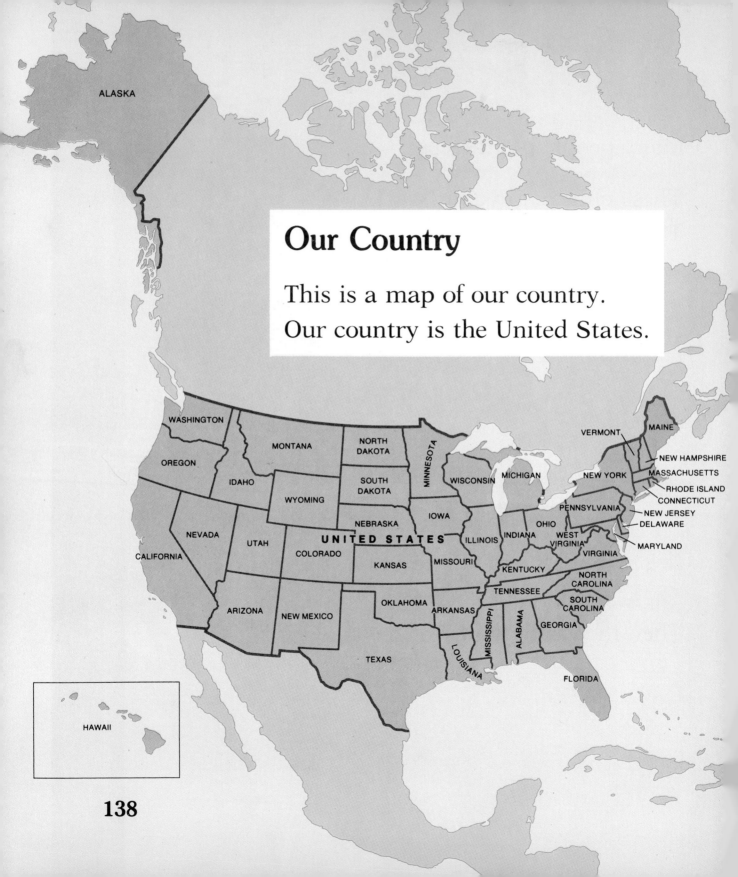

Our Country

This is a map of our country.
Our country is the United States.

138

This is our country's flag.

It has 50 stars.

It has one star for each state.

We think of our flag on Flag Day.

July 4 is a birthday.

It is the birthday of our country.

What will you do on the Fourth of July?

Words to Know

bank

globe

Earth

home

factory

lake

family

land

farm

library

fire house

map

142

money

neighborhood

ocean

police

post office

river

school

shopping center

store

water

wind

work

143

ACKNOWLEDGEMENTS

Design Credits   *Photo/Art Coordination:* Connie Komack   *Art Editing:* Penny Peters   *Photo Research:* Connie Komack
Model Coordination: Joni Cline

Cover: Gloria Karlson   *Unit Openers:* Ray H. Burns (Lee Ames & Zak, Ltd.)
Maps: Dick and John Sanderson

Illustration Credits   21, 30, 31: Joyce Dos Santos. **38–39:** Tony D'Adamo (Lee Ames & Zak, Ltd.). **51:** Andrew Z. Shiff. **60:** Tony D'Adamo (Lee Ames & Zak, Ltd.). **64–65:** Bob Priest. **68:** Joyce Dos Santos. **69:** Bob Priest. **87:** Andrew Z. Shiff. **100–103:** Joyce Dos Santos. **106–107:** Tony D'Adamo (Lee Ames & Zak, Ltd.). **123:** Bob Priest. **126–127:** A. G. Smith. **142–143:** Andrew Z. Shiff.

Photo Credits   Unit One: 10: W. K. Almond (Stock, Boston). **11:** David Muench. **12:** *t* Jonathan Rawle (Stock, Boston); *b* James A. Sugar. **13:** *t* Connie Komack; *b* J. C. Allen & Son, Inc. **14:** *t* Tom Magno; *b* Hank Morgan (Rainbow). **15:** Dan McCoy (Rainbow). **16:** Bohdan Hrynewych (Stock, Boston). **17:** *t* Jeff Gnass; *bl* Tom Walker (Stock, Boston); *br* Frank Siteman (Stock, Boston). **18:** *t* Charles E. Schmidt (Taurus Photos); *bl* John Avery; *br* Donald Deitz (Stock, Boston). **19:** William Moriarty (Rainbow). **20:** Andrew Brilliant & Carol Palmer. **22:** Kurt Scholz (Shostal Associates); *inset* E. R. Degginger. **23:** Carlye Calvin; *inset* Jen & Des Bartlett (Bruce Coleman Inc.). **24:** Fred Bruemmer. **25:** R. S. Virdee (Grant Heilman Photography). **26:** *l* Andrew Brilliant & Carol Palmer; *r* Grant Heilman Photography. **27:** *l* Clyde H. Smith (Peter Arnold, Inc.); *r* Karl Hentz (The Image Bank). **28:** *t* Don Rutledge (Taurus Photos); *b* Swiss National Tourist Office. **29:** *tl* Shostal Associates; *tr* Jack Fields (Photo Researchers, Inc.); *b* Don Smetzer (Kay Reese & Associates). **30:** *t* NASA; *ml* Stock, Boston; *mr* Tom Magno; *bl* Grant Heilman Photography; *br* Nick Passmore (Stock, Boston). **31:** Andrew Brilliant & Carol Palmer.

Unit Two: 34: *tl* L. L. T. Rhodes (Taurus Photos); *tr* Barry L. Runk (Grant Heilman Photography); *bl* Jean-Claude LeJeune (Stock, Boston); *br* Norman Prince. **35:** *tl, r* Michal Heron; *bl, r* John Lei (Stock, Boston). **36:** *tl* Orville Johnson (Camerique); *tr* Gilles Peress Magnum); *bl* Tom Stack & Associates; *br* Edith G. Haun (Stock, Boston). **37:** *tl* E. R. Degginger; *tr* Grant Heilman Photography; *bl* Paul Light (Lightwave); *br* Owen Franken (Stock, Boston). **40:** Andrew Brilliant & Carol Palmer. **41:** *t* Jacqueline Durand; *bl* Andrew Brilliant & Carol Palmer; *br* Camilla Smith (Rainbow). **42:** *l* Sam Ashey (Stock, Boston); *r* Peter Menzel (Stock, Boston). **43:** *tl, tr* John Coletti; *b* Susan Lapides. **44–49:** Andrew Brilliant & Carol Palmer. **50:** *tl* Jerry Howard (Positive Images); *tr* Don C. Arns (Tom Stack & Associates); *b* Bohdan Hrynewych (Picture Group). **51:** *l* Owen Franken (Stock, Boston); *m* W. B. Finch (Stock, Boston); *r* Charles Glen Kirk (West Stock, Inc.).

Unit Three: 54–57: Andrew Brilliant & Carol Palmer. **58:** Fredrik Bodin. **59:** *tl* Paul Light (Lightwave); *m, bl* Andrew Brilliant & Carol Palmer; *r* David P. Sheffield (Woodfin Camp & Associates). **60:** Erik Anderson (Stock, Boston). **61:** *tl* Martha Tabor; *tr* Owen Franken (Stock, Boston); *b* Joe Baker (FPG). **62–63:** Andrew Brilliant & Carol Palmer. **66:** Linda Moore (Rainbow). **67:** Jerry Howard (Positive Images). **68:** *tl* E. R. Degginger; *tr* Dan Porges (Peter Arnold, Inc.); *bl, br* Connie Komack.

Unit Four: 72–81: Andrew Brilliant & Carol Palmer. **82:** Tom McHugh (Photo Researchers, Inc.). **83:** *tl* Paul Light (Lightwave); *tr* Paula Chandoha; *bl* Tom Tracy (Photophile); *br* David S. Strickler. **84:** *l* Jerry Howard (Positive Images); *r* Michal Heron. **85:** *tl* John Coletti; *tr* Michal Heron; *bl* Peter LeGrand (Kay Reese & Associates); *br* Michal Heron. **86:** *t* Andrew Brilliant & Carol Palmer; *b* Grant Heilman Photography.

Unit Five: 90–91: Grant Heilman Photography. **91:** Erik Anderson. **92:** Grant Heilman Photography. **93:** Edward Grazda (Magnum). **94:** Alan Pitcairn (Grant Heilman Photography); *inset* Thomas Hovland (Grant Heilman Photography). **95:** Grant Heilman Photography; *inset* Frank Siteman (The Picture Cube). **96–97:** Photosix. **98–99:** *t* Courtesy of I.T.T. Continental Baking Company. **99:** *bl, r* John Urban. **102:** *l* Thomas Hovland (Grant Heilman Photography); *r* Frank Siteman (The Picture Cube).

Unit Six: 108: *l* Norman Prince; *r* Bobbi Carrey (The Picture Cube). **109:** Paul Light (Lightwave). **110:** *t* Jerry Howard (Positive Images); *b* Roger A. Clark, Jr. (Photo Researchers, Inc.). **111:** *t* Jerry Howard (Positive Images); *b* Paul Light (Lightwave). **112–113:** Andrew Brilliant & Carol Palmer. **114–115:** Lee Gordon. **116:** Andrew Brilliant & Carol Palmer. **117:** *tl* Ron Sherman (Camerique); *tr* John Urban; *b* Andrew Brilliant & Carol Palmer. **118:** Andrew Brilliant & Carol Palmer. **119:** *t* Charlie Schneider (Photophile); *b* J. DiMaggio & J. Kalish (Peter Arnold, Inc.). **120:** *l* Harry Redl (Black Star); *rt* Robert Harding Associates; *rb* Marc & Evelyne Bernheim (Woodfin Camp & Associates). **121:** *t* Michal Heron (Woodfin Camp & Associates); *b* Eric Simmons (Stock, Boston). **122:** *tl* Jerry Howard (Positive Images); *tr* Lee Gordon; *bl, br* Andrew Brilliant & Carol Palmer.

Unit Seven: 126: "Christopher Columbus" by Sebastiano del Piombo. The Metropolitan Museum of Art, gift of J. Pierpont Morgan, 1900. **128:** Jerry Howard (Positive Images). **129:** Courtesy of John Hancock Mutual Life Insurance Company. **130:** Andrew Brilliant & Carol Palmer. **131:** Rose Skytta (Jeroboam). **132:** Francis Miller (*Life Magazine*, © 1963 Time, Inc.). **133:** Courtesy of The Lincoln National Life Insurance Company and the Warren Museum. **134:** "Washington at Dorchester Heights" by Gilbert Stuart. American, 1755–1828. Oil on panel, 107½ x 71¼ in. (273 x 181 cm.), 30.76a. Deposited by the City of Boston. Courtesy of the Museum of Fine Arts, Boston. **135:** Library of Congress. **136:** Thomas Hopker (Woodfin Camp & Associates). **137:** *t* Werner Braun; *b* Tom Magno. **139:** Carl Purcell (Photo Researchers, Inc.) **140:** Brian Seed (CLICK/Chicago). **141:** J. R. Holland (Stock, Boston).